LET'S VISIT YUGOSLAVIA

27528

Let's visit
YUGOS▮▮▮▮▮

JULIAN POPESCU

BURKE

First published July 1968
Second edition October 1979
Third revised edition 1984
© Julian Popescu 1968 and 1984

ACKNOWLEDGEMENTS

The Author and Publishers are grateful to J. Allan Cash Ltd., Paul Gorjup, the Romanian Embassy, the Yugoslav Embassy and the Yugoslav National Tourist Office for permission to reproduce photographs in this book.
The cover photograph of Pocitelj on the Neretva River was supplied by Pictor International Limited.

CIP data
Popescu, Julian
  Let's visit Yugoslavia – 3rd ed.
  1. Yugoslavia – Social life and customs – Juvenile literature
  I. Title
  949.7'02   DR312
ISBN 0 222 01026 6

Burke Publishing Company Limited
Pegasus House, 116–120 Golden Lane, London EC1Y 0TL, England.
Burke Publishing (Canada) Limited
Registered Office: 20 Queen Street West, Suite 3000, Box 30, Toronto, Canada M5H 1V5.
Burke Publishing Company Inc.
Registered Office: 333 State Street, PO Box 1740, Bridgeport, Connecticut 06601, U.S.A.
Filmset in "Monophoto" Baskerville by Green Gates Studios Ltd., Hull, England.
Printed in Singapore by Tien Wah Press (Pte.) Ltd.

Contents

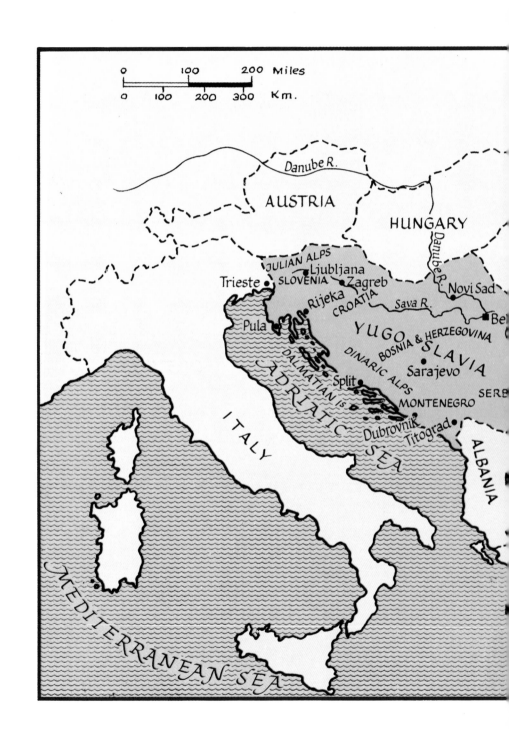

YUGOSLAVIA

U.S.S.R.

RUMANIA

IRON GATES

Danube R.

BLACK SEA

BULGARIA

je

RHODOPE MASSIF

ONIA

Vardar R.

CE

TURKEY

ATLANTIC OCEAN

EUROPE

YUGOSLAVIA

MEDITERRANEAN SEA

AFRICA

Facts and Figures on Yugoslavia

Yugoslavia is easy to find on the map for she is the largest country in south-eastern Europe with a total area of 225,500 square kilometres (99,600 square miles). She lies on the western side of the Balkan peninsula. The word Balkan is of Turkish origin and means "chain of mountains". Much of Yugoslavia is covered by mountains. Her population of

Yugoslavia has many mountain ranges such as this one—part of which is a National Park

nearly 22·5 million is made up of more than a dozen different nationalities.

The Yugoslavs (the name means "Southern Slavs") belong to the Slav family of peoples. They are related to Russians, Czechoslovaks, Poles and Bulgarians. The Yugoslavs themselves are formed of four main national groups, known as the Serbs, Croats, Slovenes and Macedonians.

The country is comparatively undeveloped, and has few tarmac roads or railways. There are still many villages and small towns which can be reached only by horse-drawn carts because the roads are so steep and difficult. The mountains are mostly uninhabited and many of the higher valleys are wild and visited only by shepherds and their flocks.

The north-eastern part of Yugoslavia is a flat plain which is dusty and hot during summer. In winter it is bitterly cold. The roads become blocked by snow, and people have to travel in sledges drawn by horses.

The western part of the country is much warmer. Here the influence of the Mediterranean Sea can be felt. The Mediterranean is never cold. The shallow ledge stretching across the Gibraltar Strait is a barrier against the cold currents of the Atlantic Ocean. This ledge, and the heat from the sun, keeps the Mediterranean warm all the year round.

Because the Yugoslavs are formed of several national groups, the country has three official languages. Serbo-Croat is the language spoken by Serbs and Croats. Slovene is spoken in the north, and Macedonian in the far south. Both these

10

A typical beach scene. Yugoslavia's coastal region, with its warm Mediterranean climate, is popular with holiday-makers

last two languages are similar to but not the same as Serbo-Croat.

The Serbs, Macedonians and other Slav peoples use the Cyrillic alphabet for writing, instead of the Latin alphabet. It was named after St Cyril, a monk who was born in Thessalonika in Greece in the early Middle Ages. St Cyril and his brother St Methodius not only taught the Slav peoples how to read and write; they also introduced them to the branch of Christianity known as the Orthodox religion.

The Croats and Slovenes, on the other hand, use the Latin alphabet. This is because their forefathers were taught by Catholic missionaries.

Yugoslav children learn to read and write in their own

language at elementary school. When they go to secondary school, they have to study all the three languages of Yugoslavia and use the two kinds of alphabet.

The majority of the population are farmers. Yugoslavia is considered an important farming country. She exports foodstuffs, wines and tobacco to all parts of the world.

The Yugoslavs buy and sell goods using money called dinars. Each dinar is made up of one hundred paras. The para is worth almost nothing: for example, it costs five paras to buy an ordinary postage stamp.

During the Second World War, the whole of Yugoslavia was occupied by the Italian and German armies, after bitter fighting. At the end of the war, Yugoslavia was a poor country. She had been used as a battlefield; many of her towns were in ruins and the land was overgrown with weeds. Farmers and their families often had to live in tents. They grew wheat and maize and kept pigs and sheep for food—just enough for their own needs. The women made their own cloth from coarse yarn which they spun on hand-looms.

Nowadays much of this has changed; factories have been built in towns all over Yugoslavia, people are paid good wages to work in them, and many farmers have left the land to become factory workers. The towns are expanding rapidly. New housing estates, complete with shops and cinemas, are being built.

The countryside, too, is going through considerable change. New bridges are being built and roads widened for the

12

There are many new factories springing up all over Yugoslavia. This picture shows plates stacked ready for despatching in a modern china factory

growing motor traffic. Where there is a water-shortage, pumps are being installed on the banks of rivers for irrigation. In the mountains, rivers are dammed to produce electricity for the new towns in the valleys and plains. Oil pipelines are being laid to connect newly discovered oilfields with refineries. The construction of gas pipelines is under way for supplying methane, or natural gas, to chemical factories and steelworks.

Yugoslavia is a Communist country but she has stayed neutral for many years now. When the Second World War ended, she joined the alliance of Communist countries in eastern and central Europe. In 1948, she quarrelled with the U.S.S.R. and the other members of this Communist alliance

13

and was expelled. Since then she has managed to maintain her independence.

There is much to learn about Yugoslavia and her people. There are mountain villages where people live without electricity, main drainage, running water, schools or shops. There are towns with Turkish mosques and street bazaars—for the Turks conquered Yugoslavia in the sixteenth century and ruled the country for over three hundred years. There are beautiful resorts by the sea with modern hotels and beaches packed with tourists. Let's visit Yugoslavia and find out more about her.

Land and Climate

To the north, east and south, Yugoslavia is surrounded by seven neighbours. To the west, she faces Italy across the Adriatic Sea. She has many islands along her western coastline. In western Yugoslavia there are ranges of high mountains and hills which extend south-eastwards across the Greek and Bulgarian borders.

Look at the map and find the big river which crosses the plains of eastern Yugoslavia. It is the Danube River which

Yugoslavia shares with Romania. Later, we shall read how the two countries have co-operated to make the Danube into an international waterway, linking the Near East with Central Europe.

The Danube River empties its waters into the Black Sea through a large swampy delta. It is Yugoslavia's most important river.

North-eastern Yugoslavia is a vast level plain, sweeping away in every direction as far as the eye can see. This area is part of the territory known as the Great Hungarian Plain. Thousands of years ago this land was under water, covered by an inland sea. Then earthquakes and earth movements gradually pushed the land up. Little by little, the Great Hungarian Plain was formed, from deposits of mud, sand and stones brought down from the mountains by rivers.

Yugoslavia's mountains are a continuation of the tall and rugged Alps which stretch in an arc across northern Italy. In the north of the country are the Julian Alps with the highest peak in Yugoslavia, Mount Triglav; shaped like a three-cornered hat, it rises to 2,863 metres (9,393 feet).

Running down the centre of Yugoslavia like a backbone are the Dinaric Alps. This mountain range cuts off the Adriatic coast from the rest of the country. To the south and west of the Dinaric Alps are the Rhodope Massif and the Balkan Mountains.

The map shows us that Yugoslavia is bordered by Italy in the west and Austria and Hungary in the north. In the east

Mount Triglav in the Julian Alps, the highest peak in Yugoslavia

Yugoslavia has frontiers with Romania and Bulgaria, while in the far south her neighbours are Greece and Albania.

Nearly three-quarters of Yugoslavia's territory is made up of mountains and hills. Some of the mountains are snow-covered all the year round. Other mountains are made of limestone worn into deep hollows, gulleys and trenches by

16

rain and wind. This region is called the Karst. Here there are many unexplored pot-holes, underground caves and streams.

It can be very hot in Yugoslavia's plains during the summer, and very cold in the winter. The average summer temperature is 22°C, or 71°F, while the average temperature in winter is 0°C, or 32°F. This means that for most of the winter the earth is frozen too hard to be ploughed by the farmers.

Yugoslavia and the other Balkan countries have similar geographical features. They have high mountains and flat plains, cold winters and hot summers. The main difference between Yugoslavia and the rest of the Balkans is in the great variety of landscape and the variation in climate from one part of the country to another. In the Adriatic region and far south the winter is mild and rainy; elsewhere winters are cold and snowy.

In fact, Yugoslavia is made up of three different types of terrain, and has three distinct kinds of climate. Firstly, there are the Dalmatian coast and islands, and the far south called the Morava-Vardar Depression. Here it is sunny and warm, with a Mediterranean climate. Secondly, there is the region of the Dinaric Alps and the Rhodope Massif; this region is cool all the year round with an Alpine and sub-Alpine climate. Thirdly, there is the plain in the north-east of the country, where it is very hot in summer and very cold in winter. (This type of climatic condition is known as "continental climate".)

The Dalmatian coast (the name given to all but the northern part of Yugoslavia's coastline) and the offshore islands are

One of the many peninsulas on the Dalmatian coast

extremely beautiful. The coast is very rocky and jagged with numerous bays and fjords. The natural scenery and the constant sunshine have made the coast popular with tourists from all over the world. There are old towns, many dating from the Middle Ages, and fishermen's villages which cater for visitors. There are wooded slopes, and terraces planted with vines, and with olive- and fig-trees. There are mulberry trees, too, and groves of oranges and lemons.

The Dalmatian islands are made of limestone, sandstone and other rock. The islands are actually the tops of mountains which sank into the sea in prehistoric times. There are hundreds of these islands forming a chain running parallel to the coast. Korcula and Hvar are the largest of these, with white and yellowish cliffs surrounded by a dazzling blue sea. The

18

autumns are unpleasant on the islands because of the winds which sweep the Adriatic: the cold wind, known as the *bora*, and the dry wind, known as the *scirocco*. But the winters are mild and the rain comes in sudden showers. The soil is poor on most of the islands and only moss-like plants, coarse grass, scrub and pine-trees grow well.

Now let's look at the map and find the Morava-Vardar Depression. This region lies in the far south of Yugoslavia near the Greek border. It is a broad valley surrounded by mountains which keep off the cold winds of the north. Because the climate here is warm all the year round, farmers can grow rice, vines and tobacco as their main crops.

The second geographical division of Yugoslavia is formed by the Dinaric Alps and Rhodope Massif which rise in places to nearly 2,500 metres (over 8,000 feet). Passes are rare, which makes travel from one region to another difficult. In winter, most of the passes are blocked by snow and ice. But in spring the snow melts, uncovering strips of pasture which the shepherds visit with flocks of sheep and goats from the valleys. The shepherds have dogs to guard their flocks because of hungry wolves. After lambing, the sheep are milked, and the milk is used for making cheese.

The climate here is too cold for many plants and trees to grow. But some Alpine flowers—blue gentians, saxifrages and dwarf poppies—grow in the pastures. Rhododendron bushes can be seen among the bare rocks. And heather and moss grow up to the region where the snow and ice begins.

It is difficult for people to live right up in the mountains because of the cold weather and barren ground; so the high mountain slopes are uninhabited except for a few shepherds and hunters. But lower down the mountain-sides, in the valleys, permanent settlements are possible. People have cleared the land of trees here and sown wheat and oats, which grow well because the land is rich in potash.

There are also valuable mineral deposits in the mountains of Yugoslavia. Lead, copper, chromium, zinc, bauxite and antimony are all mined here. Yugoslavia is the leading European country, after the U.S.S.R., in her production of lead, antimony and chromium; and she has the third largest output of copper and bauxite.

The plains of Yugoslavia in the north-east occupy a quarter of the country. The Danube River flows through the middle of the plains. In many places, low-lying land near the river is flooded after rains. That is why these lands are called "flood plains". Herds of domestic buffaloes with long, flat horns stand in the muddy water. These gentle animals are used by farmers for pulling carts.

Reeds, rushes and clumps of coarse grass grow on the flood plains. Water rats and otters live in the river banks. Beavers used to live there, too, but they were hunted to extinction for their pelts. Many wild birds search for food in the marshes and nest among the rushes. Wild duck, geese, herons and storks can all be seen. They live on snakes, frogs, small fish or water insects.

Harvesting in one of the immense fields of maize which have made this region known as "Yugoslavia's granary"

Away from the river the great plains are very fertile. This area has been called Yugoslavia's granary, and one can see vast fields of wheat and maize stretching endlessly into the distance. Apart from crops, the people here raise horses and cattle. Herds of them can be seen grazing in the meadows. The cows have long, upward-curving horns; there are tin bells round their necks which tinkle as they walk. The horses are handsome and well-bred.

21

Tall trees, such as the poplar, the elm and the acacia with its sweet-smelling flowers, grow in copses on the plains. This flat land is the home of hares, voles and dormice; hedgehogs, foxes and badgers live here, too, as well as pheasants and partridges.

In this region, the village houses have white-washed walls and thatched roofs. There are apple and plum orchards, where geese roam freely under the trees, and plantations of flax and hemp which the farmers grow for making cloth. The fibrous stalks of the flax or hemp are put in the village pond and left to soak for a fortnight before being beaten with wooden mallets. The women then comb the fibres with a curry comb, turning them into balls of fluff. They spin the fluff into a coarse yarn which they weave into cloth on a hand-loom.

Most of the transport between the villages is provided by small carts, drawn by oxen or horses. These carry grain, vegetables and fruit to the local market, returning with pots and pans and other household goods needed by the farmer.

In Yugoslavia, the dividing line between the mountains and the plains runs through hills, where there is a mixture of grassland and forest.

The dense forests are full of wildlife. Besides the animals of the plains there are wolves, wild boars and deer. Squirrels, lynxes and wild cats climb the trees.

The Middle Danube Basin

Except for the Danube and its tributaries, Yugoslavia has few major rivers due to the fact that much of the country is covered by mountains. Most Yugoslav rivers are short; they start as mountain torrents, falling over stone ledges and flowing swiftly down rocky valleys, but they dwindle quickly to shallow streams before reaching the sea. Such are the rivers on the western slopes of the Dinaric Alps which flow into the Adriatic Sea. But the north-eastern plains have the mighty Danube River which drains all the eastern slopes of the Dinaric Alps and Rhodope Massif as well as the western slopes of the Carpathian Mountains in Romania.

The Danube rises in the Schwarzwald, or Black Forest, in West Germany, high above sea level. It is over 2,810 kilo-metres (1,750 miles) long, and is the second longest river in Europe after the Volga. It crosses Austria and the Great Hungarian Plain before reaching Yugoslavia. It is very wide in places by the time it reaches the Yugoslav frontier. When the sun melts the ice and snow on the mountains in the spring, water comes pouring down the mountain sides, swelling the streams and rivers which flow into the Danube.

The most important of these tributary rivers are the Drava, the Tisa and the Sava, which joins the Danube at Belgrade, Yugoslavia's capital. Another important tributary coming from the south is the Morava. These rivers bring soil and sand which are carried down by the Danube and deposited at

23

bends, or in places where the river is sluggish. In this way, islands and sandbanks form in the middle of the river. The islands are covered with reeds and bulrushes where thousands of frogs live.

Beyond Belgrade, the Danube flows through flat, rich farmland. The river is so broad in places that one can hardly see across it. Soon it reaches the foothills of the Carpathian and Balkan Mountains, their lower slopes covered with beech trees, their higher slopes with evergreens—spruce and pines and firs.

For a stretch of 112 kilometres (seventy miles) the Danube now flows through a string of narrow gorges and basins which form the border between Yugoslavia and Romania. Navigation is difficult in the gorges because of rapids, and the rocks hidden in the river-bed. Shipping channels are marked by red buoys; but, even so, no ship's captain will negotiate them at night.

The banks on each side of the river are made of schist—a hard layered rock—and form steep walls which tower at great heights above the water. Perhaps the most spectacular part of this stretch of the Danube is the Kazan Gorge. Here the river is very narrow. It is also extremely deep, because of the existence of potholes.

On one bank of the Kazan Gorge is a winding road, built in Roman times. The Romans cut the rock away to make a passage, and bored holes in the rocky wall for beams to support the roadway.

24

The steep banks of the Kazan Gorge. The Danube becomes narrow and extremely deep at this point

Beyond the Kazan Gorge there was an island in the middle of the Danube called Ada-Kaleh. According to legend, a penniless old Turkish friar, whose name was Mishkin Baba, once roamed the earth looking for a place free from evil and misfortune. He found this island in the Danube and settled there with his friends. The legend arose because the island was, in fact, inhabited by Turks, although belonging to Romania. The islanders manufacture cigarettes, and make cakes and Turkish Delight for tourists. The men wear the traditional black-tasselled hat, known as the *fez*, and baggy trousers. The women still drape their heads and veil their faces when they appear in public.

Beyond the island of Ada-Kaleh were the Iron Gates Rapids.

25

A view of the Rasa Valley, an area of richly fertile agricultural land

Here, the current was so fast and dangerous that all ships, barges and boats had to pass through a canal built parallel with the Yugoslav bank. When the water was low, in July and August, boulders and razor-sharp rocks were visible jutting out of the swirling waters. The river looked shallow, but there were deep potholes hidden among the rocks.

A few years ago, Yugoslavia and Romania built a huge hydro-electric power station on the site of the Iron Gates Rapids. The scheme involved building a powerful dam across these rapids. Once this was completed, the waters rose behind the dam, engulfing the island of Ada-Kaleh and several

26

villages on the Yugoslav and Romanian banks. (But before that happened, the inhabitants were, of course, given new homes.) Locks were constructed alongside the dam to allow shipping to go through. And navigation through the gorges became easier because the level of the water was kept constantly high. Now the building of a second dam across the Danube has been planned by the two countries.

The Danube and its tributaries mean a great deal to the country. They provide water for livestock and for irrigation, making the fields of Yugoslavia capable of producing rich crops of melons, cucumbers, tomatoes and other vegetables. They also contain fish of all kinds.

The Danube, in addition, is an important line of communication between the Rhine valley, Central Europe and the countries of the Near East. Because of the fact that it carries so much international traffic, it is considered a free waterway. A central authority regulates navigation and keeps international control of the river. The authority is composed of all the countries (with the exception of Germany) through which the Danube passes—Austria, Hungary, Czechoslovakia, Yugoslavia, Romania, Bulgaria and the U.S.S.R.

River steamers and barges can travel along most of the Danube except during the winter when the river may be blocked by ice. Yugoslav barges carry cargo such as wheat, timber and minerals to ports in Hungary and Austria and come back laden with manufactured goods.

The Six Republics

Yugoslavia is a Socialist Federal Republic. This means that there is a federal government and a federal assembly governing the whole of Yugoslavia. Within this framework, the country is divided into six provinces, or Republics. Each Republic has a government of its own with an assembly or parliament to run its affairs. It also has its own official language. Recently each Republic was given the right to run and maintain a regular army, although the Federal Government is still responsible for calling people up into the national army in times of emergency.

The Head of State is the President of the Federal Republic. He is chosen by the Federal Assembly. The Federal Assembly

President Josip Broz Tito as a young man

chose Josip Broz Tito as their first President, an office which he held for the remainder of his long life. After Tito's death in 1980, a new President was elected. But the country is now governed by a group of men and women (elected by the Communist Party), rather than by one man.

The names of the six Republics are: Slovenia; Croatia; Serbia; Bosnia and Herzegovina; Montenegro; Macedonia.

Slovenia, bordering on Italy and Austria, lies in the extreme north of Yugoslavia. The Sava River runs right through the middle of the country and through high mountains.

The inhabitants are men of the mountains; this means that they are sturdy and industrious. The people of this Republic enjoy the highest standard of living in Yugoslavia and their work accounts for nearly twenty per cent of the whole country's export trade.

Slovenia is only 20,250 square kilometres (7,820 square miles) in area and the population is nearly 1,900,000. The capital is Ljubljana, a beautiful city with a Catholic cathedral and many churches (the people are Catholic) set in a valley surrounded by hills and snow-capped mountains. Ljubljana is Slovenia's most important manufacturing town. Its inhabitants find plenty of work in paper mills, furniture factories and breweries. Near by there are quarries and brickfields.

South-west of Slovenia is the Socialist Republic of Croatia. This Republic has an area of over 56,500 square kilometres (about 21,800 square miles). It lies partly in the plain and partly on the Adriatic coast, and includes most of the offshore islands. Cutting through the centre of Croatia are the Dinaric Alps.

The 4·6 million people of Croatia are Roman Catholics. Many of those living on the Adriatic coast are fishermen and seafaring people. Their main fishing grounds are in the Adriatic Sea. They also work in the shipyards and docks. The holiday resorts along the coast provide work for people in hotels, cafés and shops. The Croats living in the plain are mostly farmers.

Croatia's capital is Zagreb, a town of well over 700,000 inhabitants. In addition to factories for textiles, furniture and chemicals, Zagreb has a vast exhibition site where international trade fairs are held.

The Socialist Republic of Serbia lies east of Slovenia and Croatia and is bordered by Hungary to the north and Romania to the east. Much of the country is flat but there are some high mountains in the south and west.

Serbia was conquered by the Turks in the Middle Ages and they inflicted great suffering on the people. After several uprisings, which were cruelly put down by the Turks, the Serbs gained semi-independence. At first their country was very small, but it increased as the Turks lost more wars and territories. Today, Serbia is the largest Republic in Yugoslavia. It has an area of 88, 360 square kilometres (34,115 square miles) and a population of over 9·2 million. This includes nearly half a million Hungarian and Romanian settlers who live in the plain east of the Danube. Serbia contains the capital of Yugoslavia, Belgrade, and two self-governing provinces named Vojvodina and Kosovo.

The people of Serbia belong to the Eastern Orthodox Church. They are very religious and proud of their country. The Serbs make the sign of the cross whenever they pass in front of a church. The Serb farmers cross themselves before they start ploughing a field or doing any other important job.

The thick forests of southern Serbia provide work for lumbermen; and there is copper to be mined in the mountains. The main crops of the region are maize, wheat and barley.

Westwards from Serbia is the Socialist Republic of Bosnia and Herzegovina. This Republic is mostly mountainous—the Dinaric Alps run down the middle of it—and heavily wooded. It has an area of 51,130 square kilometres (19,740 square miles) and a population of 4,100,000. The Bosnians and

These heavily wooded slopes are typical of the rich forest-land found throughout Bosnia and Herzegovina

Herzegovinians are a mixture of Serb and Croat with some Turkish blood. The Turkish conquerors introduced the Muslim relition, and today Christians and Muslims live side by side.

Bosnia has rich forest-lands and many coal mines. There are farms in the valleys and in areas where the forest-land has been cleared. In Herzegovina, where much of the land is composed of porous limestone, farmers grow their crops in an unusual way. After the heavy spring rains, big lakes form. But because the limestone is porous, the rainwater quickly sinks into it, leaving behind a thin layer of red earth on the rocky bed. The farmers break up the red earth with pointed sticks and plant their crops. The earth is so fertile that two or three crops can be harvested in one year.

The capital of the Republic is Sarajevo, which became famous in history on the eve of the First World War. The Austrian Archduke Francis Ferdinand was visiting Sarajevo when he was shot and fatally wounded by a Bosnian student. The Archduke's death led the Emperor of Austria to declare war on Serbia and the First World War began.

Sarajevo means "city of palaces". In the old part of the city there are large Turkish houses and two magnificent mosques built by the Turkish conquerors in the Middle Ages. Today Sarajevo is a modern city with a population of 448,000, which makes it the fourth largest in Yugoslavia. It has engineering, textile and leather factories, timber yards and brick works.

A view of Sarajevo, the "city of palaces". Note the tall, slender minarets, built by the Muslim Turks in the Middle Ages for calling the faithful to prayer

South of Bosnia and Herzegovina is the Socialist Republic of Montenegro (meaning "the Black Mountain"). This is the smallest of the six Republics with an area of only 13,812 square kilometres (5,333 square miles) and a population of nearly 600,000.

According to legend, when God made the world He found at the end of the day that He still had a bag full of rocks. He scattered the rocks on some waste-land and Montenegro was born. She occupies the southern part of Yugoslavia's Adriatic coast and borders on Lake Scutari and Albania to the south.

Her mountains are barren. You can travel for long stretches without seeing a tree, just bare limestone rocks and scrub. The

33

Adriatic coast has bays and inlets with steep cliffs on either side. Much of the coast is uninhabited but where there are settlements, farmers have terraced the hills to grow olive trees, vines and maize.

The Montenegrins are of Serb origin and belong to the Orthodox Church. Because of their steep and barren mountains they were never conquered by the Turks. They are poor and backward and barely make a living from rearing sheep and goats. The capital of Montenegro, Titograd, is built high in the mountains. It has a population of nearly 100,000.

In the early spring of 1979, terrible earthquakes rocked the towns and villages of Montenegro. Roads and bridges caved in and many houses, tourist hotels and other public buildings collapsed, killing hundreds of people and leaving thousands without shelter.

Yugoslavia's sixth republic is Macedonia, which lies in the far south of the country and is bordered by Albania in the west, Greece in the south and Bulgaria in the east.

Macedonia has an area of 25,713 square kilometres (over 9,900 square miles) and a population of nearly 1,914,000.

The Macedonians are a mixture of Serb and Bulgarian. They are very proud and independent people. They like to call themselves Macedonians and feel different from the other peoples of Yugoslavia. For many years, Macedonia was a Bulgarian province and the Bulgarians still consider it should belong to them.

Macedonia's main river is the Vardar. Because of the dry

Sheep grazing on the rocky slopes typical of Montenegro

summers, the waters of the Vardar are used for irrigation. Cereals, tobacco, grapes and cotton are grown in the Vardar valley, the Republic's main farming region. Macedonia also has mineral wealth in the mountains—chromium, antimony and manganese are mined here.

Skopje, the capital of Macedonia, is a very ancient city. Before Roman times it was the capital of the kingdom of Dardania. The Romans conquered the city in the second century A.D. and the Roman Emperor Justinian was born here in the fifth century. Then the Turkish armies marched through to conquer most of the Balkans. The Turks intro-

These houses on the outskirts of Skopje were built to give temporary shelter to the townspeople who lost their homes as a result of the earthquake

duced their mosques, bazaars, and narrow streets with overhanging houses into the city. It has a population of 503,000.

Today, Skopje has been almost completely rebuilt. This is because in 1963 most of the town was destroyed by an earthquake, in which over one thousand people lost their lives. Now Skopje is the third largest city in Yugoslavia with factories for textiles, chemicals, tobacco, food and leather goods.

36

Early History

About 2,500 years ago the plains and valleys of present-day Yugoslavia were inhabited by a tribe of wild, nomadic people called Illyrians. These people made their way across the mountains as far west as the Adriatic coast. There, they took to piracy, plundering Roman ships and crossing the sea to raid settlements on the opposite shore, which today is part of Italy.

The Romans at first killed all Illyrian pirates they caught alive; but the raids continued. So the Roman legions crossed the Adriatic and conquered part of the land of the Illyrians in the third century B.C.

Later, the whole country was turned into a Roman province by the Emperor Tiberius. The Romans built towns and roads and brought settlers to till the land. The people became rich and happy.

But the law and order brought by the Romans to the ancient land of the Illyrians did not last long. Hordes of barbarian invaders came from the north and east, ransacking settlements, and forcing the Romans to withdraw. Then in the fifth century A.D. a tribe of Mongolian invaders called Huns swept the plains, destroying everything in their path. The Huns were good horsemen but they were barbaric and very cruel. They even ate the people they killed. Most of the former Roman province of Illyria was destroyed and deserted after the Huns left.

Towards the end of the sixth century A.D. groups of nomadic people called Slavs came and settled in the Middle Danube valley. One small group called Slovenes settled in the north of present-day Yugoslavia. Another larger group of Slavs, known as Croats, settled farther south. The most numerous group, who settled in the plains and valleys of the extreme south, were called Serbs. Because these Slav peoples came to southern Europe they were called Southern Slavs, or "Yugoslavs". (The word *yug* means "southern" in the old Slavonic language.)

The Yugoslavs farmed the fertile lands and established settlements. They built wooden huts with thatched roofs and surrounded their villages by ditches and wooden fences. They owned cattle and pigs and cultivated wheat and barley on the common land. The elders of the community decided what work each man should do. No person could marry without their permission.

The more adventurous Yugoslavs pushed westwards and crossed the mountains, eventually reaching the Adriatic coast. Other Yugoslavs migrated southwards as far as the Greek and Albanian borders.

During the early Middle Ages the Slovenes and Croats came under the influence of Bavarian rulers and missionaries (from what is now southern Germany), who introduced the Roman Catholic religion into the country. Living farther south, the Serbs and Macedonians were converted to the Eastern Orthodox Church, and were dominated by the Byzantine Empire.

The ancient town of Mostar where the Turks made their headquarters after conquering Herzegovina

Thus, at an early stage in their history the Yugoslav peoples came under different foreign rulers and belonged to different churches. The deep religious division between the Yugoslav peoples has lasted to the present day. In addition, their separate ways of life and traditions have made them often

39

disagree with each other, and for many years prevented their union.

In 1453 Constantinople, the capital of the Byzantine Empire, was besieged and captured by the Ottoman Turks. Soon the Turkish armies, on horse and foot, advanced into the Balkans and conquered most of the lands of the Yugoslav peoples. The Turkish soldiers were well armed; with their curved swords, shields and spears they were unconquerable. The Turks established their Ottoman Empire, where once the Byzantines had been the masters. They ruled Macedonians, Serbs, Bosnians and many other peoples for centuries. The

This bridge was built in the sixteenth century by the Turkish conquerors, and is just one of the many legacies of Turkish rule to be seen throughout Yugoslavia

Slovenes and Croats of the north, although suffering from the constant raids of Turkish marauders, escaped from Turkish rule.

From the seventeenth century onwards, the Ottoman Empire began to decline and lose, one by one, the lands it had conquered. It had powerful enemies in Austria and Hungary (which was then the Austro-Hungarian Empire), and in Russia. These powers wanted to drive the Turkish armies out of the Balkan countries. They were helped by the fact that the people whom the Turks had conquered often rose up against their rulers. In 1821, the Serbs were given semi-independence by the Turks, who continued, however, to keep troops in the main towns. About fifty years later, these troops were withdrawn and the Serbs became fully independent. In the next chapter we shall see how the Serbs and the other Yugoslav peoples succeeded in becoming united as one kingdom.

Two World Wars

At the turn of the nineteenth century, much of present-day Yugoslavia was ruled by the Austro-Hungarian Empire. Amongst the Yugoslavs, the Serbs were the only people to have an independent sovereign state. The other Yugoslav

41

peoples were living under foreign rule; but they desired independence, and wanted to unite themselves with Serbia. The Austro-Hungarian rulers, however, were determined to prevent this union. They did not want to lose their territories.

We have learned how the Austrian Archduke Francis Ferdinand was murdered when visiting Sarajevo. This incident gave Austro-Hungary an excuse for sending Serbia an ultimatum and then declaring war on her in 1914. This was the beginning of the First World War. Great Britain and France joined the war on the side of Serbia. Germany and Turkey came in on the side of Austro-Hungary. Soon, nearly all the countries in Europe were fighting.

The war ended in defeat for Germany and Austro-Hungary. And at last the Yugoslav peoples were given the chance to unite.

In the winter of 1919 the act of union was proclaimed and Yugoslavia was officially born. She was called the Kingdom of Serbs, Croats and Slovenes.

However, this was not the end of the Slav peoples' troubles. In 1941, two years after the beginning of the Second World War, Germany and Italy invaded Yugoslavia. The Yugoslavs resisted the invaders for as long as they could. But at last they were defeated. Thousands of Yugoslav soldiers escaped to the forests and mountains. They became guerilla fighters. Some of these guerillas were Communists. Others were royalists.

At first, Communists and royalists fought side by side. But later they began to fight one another. So, in addition to enemy

42

This photograph of Yugoslav school children was taken during the Second World War. Their ragged clothes and bare feet give an indication of the poverty of the people at that time

occupation, the country suffered a civil war. To make matters worse, some Yugoslavs collaborated with the Germans and betrayed their fellow-countrymen.

At last, in the autumn of 1944, the Russian army reached the Yugoslav border. They entered the country and drove the Germans out, with the help of the Communist guerillas. The Yugoslavs were free from German occupation. But they had lost over a million and a half men as a result of the war. Of these, half a million had died in the civil war between royalists and Communists.

This time, many Yugoslavs felt that the Kingdom of Serbs,

43

Yugoslav guerillas during a lull in the fighting against the Germans

Croats and Slovenes should become a republic. The Communists were in favour of a republic, the royalists wanted a monarchy. The Communists prevailed, and in 1945 Marshal Josip Broz Tito, the leader of the Communist guerilla fighters, became the head of the new Socialist Federal Republic of Yugoslavia.

After the proclamation of the Republic, the government decided that the country must have a new flag. The flag, the design of which was laid down in the country's constitution, is divided horizontally into three bands—blue, white and red—and has a large red star in the centre.

During the years which followed the end of the Second World War the Yugoslav government had to deal with major foreign policy problems. Yugoslavia had joined an alliance of Communist countries, known as "the Cominform". This alliance was controlled by the U.S.S.R., who wished to advise the Yugoslavs on how to run their country and train their army. In addition, the U.S.S.R. bought raw materials from the Yugoslavs at very low prices. The Yugoslavs felt that they should develop their own industries, and that they should be paid better prices for their raw materials. So Yugoslavia's relations with the U.S.S.R. grew worse. In 1948 Marshal Stalin, leader of the U.S.S.R., quarrelled with Marshal Tito and expelled Yugoslavia from the Cominform. The U.S.S.R. and other Communist countries belonging to the Cominform started an economic blockade of Yugoslavia, hoping that her people would get rid of Marshal Tito. The United States of America and Great Britain realized that the independence of Yugoslavia was threatened. They immediately sent economic aid to the Yugoslav government and helped the country to overcome the difficulties caused by the Russian blockade. After Marshal Stalin's death in 1953 the blockade was lifted and the new Russian leaders again became friendly with Yugoslavia.

Industries and Resources

At the end of the Second World War, the Yugoslavs found themselves faced with shortages of every kind. Their houses and factories were in ruins; their crops of wheat and maize had been destroyed by the retreating German armies.

Food was scarce and expensive, and there were hardly any clothes or ordinary household goods to be bought in the shops.

In southern Yugoslavia there are still many traditional craftsmen. This picture shows a coppersmith at work

One of the most urgent tasks which faced the Yugoslav Federal Government was to get industrial production going again. Plans were made for building new factories and for training people in industrial skills. At this time only about ten per cent of the working population were employed in industry. Soon, many farm-workers were giving up their jobs on the land to go and work in the new factories. Tall blocks of flats and housing estates were erected on the outskirts of towns. Gradually Yugoslavia began to change from a farming nation into an industrial nation. Today, over one-third of the Yugoslav people work in factories and mines.

Yugoslavia has many minerals in her earth, but unfortunately she does not have enough coal of the kind needed for industry. She has to import coking-coal for her iron and steel plants. These plants are mostly situated in the industrial ports on the Adriatic seaboard or in the big towns of the north-eastern plain.

Southern Yugoslavia is much less industrialized than the north of the country. There are some important mines, where valuable metals such as copper, lead, chrome and zinc are extracted, but few factories. Most of the people farm plots of land or work as craftsmen in small shops or bazaars. They are poor, and their living standards are low.

The people on the Adriatic seaboard, by contrast with their brothers in the south, enjoy a high standard of living. This is because of the many industries which have been introduced into this coastal region.

A coal mine near Pula, in the northern part of Yugoslavia. The mine
has its own harbour and the photograph shows ships being loaded
with coal

There are three important ports along Yugoslavia's coastline: Split; Rijeka, which is farther north than Split; and
Pula (which used to belong to Italy). These three ports have
developed rapidly during the last few years. They now have
huge ship-building and repair yards, equipped with modern
machinery. Cargo boats, passenger liners, and large tankers,

are all built in these yards by Yugoslav workers. In addition to the shipyards, there are factories making diesel engines, turbines and boilers. There are also light-engineering factories, railway workshops and chemical plants. Rijeka has an oil refinery and extensive shunting yards and docks which now handle most of Yugoslavia's seaborne exports and imports.

Yugoslav geologists have been prospecting for oil along the coast and in the Adriatic Sea. They have found several oil-fields which may contain vast quantities of oil. If this proves to be the case, Yugoslavia will be provided with all the oil she needs, and a surplus which she can export.

Now let's pay a visit to Yugoslavia's plain in the north-east

The Split shipyard on the Dalmatian coast. This is one of the three major shipyards in Yugoslavia

of the country. As you travel across the flat land you see an industrial town far away in the distance. At first all you can see is a hazy black cloud on the horizon. This is a mixture of dust and smoke from factory chimneys, which hangs like mist in the air. As you draw nearer you see the tops of factory chimneys, radio masts, tall buildings, church spires and gas works. At last you see the whole town clearly outlined on the horizon. It is Novi Sad, now the capital of the self-governing province of Vojvodina, which stands on the left bank of the Danube. Here the Yugoslavs have developed a vast textile industry. The spinning and weaving mills of Novi Sad use the fibres of flax and hemp, which are grown near by, as well as cotton, which is brought from the far south. Some mills make their cloths of wool and silk, supplied by local farmers. Recently, in addition to the vegetable and animal fibres, the mills have started using synthetic fibres which are derived from coal and oil.

This swimming-pool was built especially for the workers of a cellulose factory in the north of Yugoslavia

The textiles made at Novi Sad are sent by rail to Belgrade and, from there, to all parts of Yugoslavia. Some are also sent by rail across the border to Budapest in Hungary.

We have mentioned the new oilfields discovered along the Adriatic Coast. Oil and methane gas are already being extracted from the plain, at Sisak in Croatia. Both the oil and gas are carried through pipelines to refineries and chemical plants at Novi Sad and Zagreb. Pipelines are now being laid from towns on the River Danube to the new industrial centres of the plain. Oil for these pipelines is brought in tankers up the Danube from the rich oilfields of Romania.

Yugoslavia does not rely entirely on oil as a source of power. We have already read that a new hydro-electric power station is being built at the Iron Gates on the Danube. It is interesting to see what effect this new scheme for producing electricity will have on the country as a whole.

High tension wires will link the power station on the Danube, across rugged mountains, with towns and mines in southern Serbia and Macedonia, great distances away. New factories will be built in these towns to use the large supply of cheap electricity. Railways will become electrified, making travel cheaper. Increased production will bring prosperity to this under-developed part of Yugoslavia. It is for these reasons that such a big and expensive power station is being developed.

The country's first atomic power-station was built in Slovenia and started to function in 1981.

Forests and Fisheries

About twenty-five per cent of Yugoslavia's territory is covered by forest. Fifty or sixty years ago the area of forest-land was much larger. Each year, timber is cut for export, industry, transport and for use as firewood. There are mountains in Bosnia which were once famous for their rich forests. Timber was cut, but no new trees were planted. The trees had helped to keep the soil firm. Now, when the rain-swollen streams swept down the mountainside they washed the topsoil away. As a result, the land became barren and deserted.

Nowadays, whenever timber is cut new trees are planted. Forest nurseries have been set up by the government near Split on the Adriatic coast. The seedlings which are grown there are sent in their thousands to all parts of Yugoslavia to replace the trees that are being cut; in this way, the seedling trees will provide the forests and the timber of the future.

The forests of Slovenia are the most valuable in the whole country. Coniferous trees such as Austrian pine, Norway spruce and silver fir grow there in abundance. These trees provide soft timber, which is used by the furniture and building industries. Soft wood is also used for telegraph poles and for making pulp and paper.

In the Sava valley there are great forests of beech and peduncular oak which grow very straight and reach a height of about 24 metres (80 feet). The timber felled here is used for making pit props and sleepers for railways.

Timber hauliers remove the logs from the forest, using teams of oxen or horses to haul them over rough ground. When they reach the road, the logs are loaded onto wagons drawn by tractors or horses.

A much simpler method of transporting logs is to float them down a river. The Sava River is frequently used for floating logs to saw-mills. Men lash the logs together into a raft. They build a makeshift cabin on the raft, since the journey may last several days. Then these men, who have to be both tough and skilled, steer the logs down the river, using huge oars to guide them past treacherous boulders and bends. At night they moor the rafts. They make a fire on the bank to cook

A raft of logs being floated down river

their supper, and tell each other stories to pass the time. Finally they reach the saw-mills and stack the logs on high ground to dry.

Commercial fishing is carried on on a small scale by Yugoslav fishermen, because the Adriatic Sea is not rich in fish. The most important fish caught along the Adriatic coast are sardines and tunny—a large relative of the mackerel which can weigh 360 kilogrammes (about 800 pounds). Shoals of this

Fishing-boats moored in the harbour at Rovinj

big fish are always on the move. When a shoal is sighted the
fishermen come out in their boats and steer the fish into an
enclosure surrounded by nets. The cornered tunny are then
stunned with sharp poles or gaffs, before being hauled aboard.
Yugoslav fishermen also catch red mullet and swimming-crab
by towing a trawl-net between two boats. They land their
catches at Rijeka or lower down the coast at Split and
Dubrovnik.

The main rivers and lakes of Yugoslavia are rich in fish.
The fishermen work mostly from the banks. They use large
nets, spread out at the end of long poles, which they dip into
the water. On good days, they may draw up the nets with a
catch of pike, smelt or perch inside.

How the Country is Farmed

Yugoslavia is a country of small farms. Yugoslavs like to own their own land and their own livestock and many people live by farming. Although some farmers have tractors, most of them still plough their fields with oxen, buffaloes or horses.

Yugoslavia is one of Europe's largest maize and wheat producers. More maize is grown than any other cereal because the crop has a high yield. Farmers eat a great deal of maize-pudding instead of bread. The plains of Serbia with their rich black topsoil are the leading producers of maize, wheat and barley.

Some Yugoslav farmers prefer to work on co-operative farms. Ten per cent of Yugoslavia's arable land—land suitable for ploughing—belongs to the co-operative farms. The largest and best co-operatives in the country are in the north-eastern

Combine harvesters at work on a farm in the plains of Serbia. This is a co-operative farm—the ordinary farmer cannot afford such expensive machinery

plains. Many of these farms once belonged to German settlers, who fled the country at the end of the Second World War, fearing that the Yugoslav guerillas and Russian soldiers would take revenge on them. Their land was taken over by the State and turned into co-operative farms on which poor Yugoslav families were re-settled.

The co-operative farms in Yugoslavia are managed in the same way as those of the U.S.S.R. The farm workers elect a committee headed by a chairman who must be a member of the Communist party. The chairman decides on the day's work and how it will be divided amongst his work-force. Like the manager of a factory, he appoints overseers and foremen. The farm committee decides what wages will be paid to the workers. The wages are paid partly in cash and partly in kind. The committee also decides on the purchase of stores, tools, fertilizers and machines. The collective farms can afford modern machinery. Huge tractors are used for ploughing the fields. Combine-harvesters cut wheat, barley and grass for seed. Even the cobs of maize are harvested by mechanical pickers.

In the autumn a general meeting is held at which the farm produce is divided up. Most of the crops have to be sold to the government at fixed prices. Some are kept for seed and the rest is shared out among the workers.

The income from the farm is used for paying wages and for farm improvements, insurance and pensions, club-houses, libraries, films and other amenities. The co-operative farm

Corn cobs hanging up to dry after the maize harvest in Croatia

workers have a higher income than some of the farmers who work their own small plot of land.

Some of the co-operative farms specialize in vegetable and fruit-growing. They have glasshouses in which they grow early potatoes, tomatoes, cucumbers and asparagus, for export. The orchards have apricot, plum and apple trees. Other farms rear pigs, cattle, sheep and poultry.

The greatest worry of farmers in Yugoslavia is the weather. Too little rain means drought and crop failure. Too much rain, especially in spring, causes the Danube and other rivers to burst their banks and flood the countryside. Crops are destroyed and livestock drowned. A hard frost in late spring can badly damage fruit crops and plants like maize and tobacco.

Pests are another great enemy of the Yugoslav farmers. There was a plague of mice in Bosnia in 1967. Millions of mice formed a column and advanced across Bosnia, eating the crops. Cats were afraid to attack them. Farmers had to

These racks are used for drying hay in Slovenia

put down poison and to use other pest-control methods to get rid of them.

Serbia and Croatia are the leading producers of sugar-beet. Farmers like to grow sugar-beet because it is so profitable. The tops of the sugar-beet are used for feeding cattle; the rest is sent to the sugar factories. When the sugar has been extracted, the pulp is returned from the factory and is used for feeding pigs and cattle.

Plums are a major fruit crop. The orchards produce sweet, reddish plums which are dried in special ovens and then exported as prunes. Yugoslavia is one of the world's leading exporters of prunes. But much of the plum crop, including windfalls and rejects from prune-making, is put to ferment in vats. The fermented pulp is distilled and turned into a strong brandy called *slivovica*, the national drink of the Yugoslavs.

Tobacco is grown on a large scale in Macedonia. Tobacco plantations are controlled by the local government. Farmers apply for a licence to grow the tobacco. Their whole crop must be delivered to the State tobacco company which is the only firm in Yugoslavia allowed to make and sell cigarettes. Other main crops produced in Macedonia are rye, wheat, maize and cotton. Rice is also grown, with the aid of irrigation—for Macedonia's summers are hot and dry.

Yugoslav farmers grow all their own food. They keep bees for honey. They also breed silk worms. The silk worms are fed on the leaves of mulberry trees. The white and black mulberry berries are a favourite fruit, and are often used for

Rice being cultivated in Macedonia. As the rice seedlings need to be grown in water, the fields are flooded artificially with river water

making jam, too. The farmers also grow green peppers, cucumbers, tomatoes and melons in their gardens.

The farmers of Montenegro and Bosnia, who live in hilly country or in the mountains, have a harder life than the farmers in the plains or valleys. Often their land has poor soil and the crops of rye, wheat and maize are small—sometimes not even big enough for their own domestic needs. Many farmers rear sheep and goats which they milk to make cheese. They sell the cheese and so add a little more to their income.

Vineyards cover vast areas in the hills and valleys of Slovenia, Croatia and Dalmatia. The vineyards are quite small; some have been planted in terraces on sunny mountain slopes. The villagers depend on the grape harvests for their livelihood.

A proportion of the grapes are picked for eating. The fruit

A modern farm cart, pulled by bullocks

is harvested by hand, packed in crates and sent to the nearest town for local marketing or for export. But most of the grape harvest is used for making wine. The grapes are usually taken to the mechanical presses where the juice is squeezed out. In remote districts where there are no mechanical presses, men, women and children press out the juice with their bare feet. Some vineyard owners believe the best wine is made in this way, since only the best juice is squeezed out by the trampling

62

of the feet. Many bottles of fine Yugoslav wines are exported to Britain and other countries.

One of Yugoslavia's more unusual crops is the sunflower. Rows of these huge yellow flowers can be seen growing in the fields, their heads about the size of bicycle wheels. The farmers leave them to go to seed. Then they gather the seeds and sell them to factories which extract oil from them. This oil is used for cooking. The seeds are also sold in packets in shops for eating, in much the same way as we might eat peanuts.

Another plant grown for its seed is the pumpkin. It is a big, round vegetable belonging to the same family as the marrow. In Yugoslavia, pumpkins are planted among maize. After the

A field of sunflowers, a common sight in the Yugoslav countryside

An unusual crop: poppy seeds being harvested in Macedonia

maize is harvested the pumpkins are left on the ground to ripen. They are then cut open and the seed is taken out, dried and salted. The rest of the pumpkin is fed to pigs.

There are several "farm laboratories" in Yugoslavia where scientists experiment with cereals and other crops. They have already succeeded in producing hardier varieties of wheat and maize which can grow at higher altitudes where the summer is short and the weather cool. In this way farmers will be able to grow crops on hills and mountains that were considered unproductive until now.

Farming in Yugoslavia is becoming a skilled occupation. Boys and girls are now able to acquire a training in various branches of agriculture at farm institutes in Belgrade, Zagreb

64

and other big cities. These institutes provide courses in agricultural engineering, dairy farming, poultry keeping, horticulture and many other subjects.

Village Life

Let us now visit a village in the heart of Serbia. It is situated in the Banat Plain in the eastern part of the country. The road leading to the village is made of tarmac, and is flanked by tall poplars. There are no hedges, and the country all around is flat. Before you enter the village you come to a crossroads. A white road-sign points to the right. It reads: *Novi Sad* 80 *km.*

In summer there is little rain in the Banat Plain. The rivers shrink and sometimes dry up altogether. Water is precious for the people of the village. All their water comes from wells, made by boring a deep hole into the ground. Water is drawn from the well in a wooden bucket fixed to the end of a long rope. The rope is tied to a pole, which is balanced like a seesaw with a heavy stone attached to the other end of it. The bucket is lowered by hand into the well. When it is full of water it is pulled up. The weighted pole holds the bucket suspended in the air while it is emptied.

The main village street is paved with cobblestones. On each

side of the street are raised banks made of earth for people to walk along. A few spindly acacia trees grow along these banks. All the other roads in the village are bumpy earth tracks. In dry weather the tracks are dusty; in wet weather they are so muddy that carts or lorries sink up to their axles in the mud.

In the centre of the village are the town hall, the post office with its blue letterbox, and the school, surrounded by a tall fence of wire netting. There is also a shop selling groceries and hardware and, next to it, an inn with a garden at the back where customers can drink *slivovica*, beer or wine in the open air.

Most of the cottages in this Serbian village are white-washed. Some are made of sun-dried bricks, called adobes. The adobes are made by hand from mud and chopped straw. The cottages have thatched roofs. There are also some houses faced with brightly painted plaster; their roofs are tiled and the gable-ends are decorated. Most of the houses have a balcony or a narrow verandah, with a bench where people can sit and chat in the evenings.

The typical Serb house has small double windows and wooden shutters. The outside windows are made of wire mesh to keep out flies and let in the air. So the rooms are dark and cool in summer. The kitchen has an open-hearth fire over which dangles a big copper cauldron. Water is heated in this cauldron. There are smaller cauldrons on the shelf for cooking food.

Most of the cottages have two or three rooms, with simple

hand-made furniture. There are coloured carpets and rugs on the floor and on the walls. Earthenware jugs and plates with flowers or patterns painted on them hang from beams in the ceiling. The best room in the house is the dining-room with a long, polished table and many chairs and benches. One room is kept as a guest room. Parents and children live and sleep together in one big room next to the kitchen.

Serb houses have no front gardens. At the back of each house there is a yard where the domestic animals—oxen, cows and horses—are kept. Some families keep a buffalo cow which gives rich, creamy milk. In one corner of the yard are the farm carts. In another is a barn. It is made of wicker and rests on wooden piles. It is used for storing maize cobs. Underneath the barn is the pigsty and next to it a henhouse. The hens and pigs are allowed to roam freely about the yard and even on the road outside. Poorer people in the village keep their young animals in the house. Lambs, kids and puppies live with the family.

Behind the yard, carefully fenced off, is the vegetable garden. The villagers grow all their own fruit and vegetables, including bright red chillies, lentils and purple, shiny-skinned aubergines which are delicious when cooked in olive oil with onion and tomato.

Most of the people who live in the village are farmers. They are rough and hardy men who work in the fields from dawn to dusk. The women are hard workers, too. In addition to all their housework, they prepare pickles, preserve fruit and make

A country boy from Slovenia, playing a local musical instrument. Note the homespun material of his shirt, which is made of hemp cloth

jams for the winter. At harvest time they take the food to the men in the fields and help cut the wheat or pick the cobs of maize.

The village carpenter is kept busy making furniture and window frames, or repairing carts. The village also has a blacksmith who shoes the horses and oxen. One of the most important people in the village is the priest. All the villagers are regular churchgoers and keep every religious festival throughout the year. They often ask the priest to pray for their dead and to bless their homes and crops. But they are superstitious, too. If there is a prolonged drought and the

68

crops are in danger, they ask gypsy children to perform a dance in skirts made of leaves. The dancing children are then splashed with water. The farmers believe that rain will soon come after this ritual dance has been performed.

A few days before Christmas every household in the village kills a pig. For weeks afterwards everybody has plenty of pork and sausages to eat. The meat keeps well because the weather is always very cold in December and January.

Now let's go to the mountains of northern Yugoslavia and learn about a village in Slovenia. There, the mountains rise to high and rugged peaks covered with snow for most of the year. Forests of dark green pine and spruce cover the valleys. Above are Alpine pastures where sheep, goats and cattle crop the tender grass.

The village is situated in a valley of the Julian Alps. Great steel cables span the valley and a foaming river plunges down a steep ravine. The village is a cluster of houses set at the foot of a cliff. The houses look like Swiss chalets. They are tall, two-storey buildings, with an attic at the top. The lower half of each house is built of large stones while the upper half is of timber. The roof is steeply pitched so that the heavy snow can slide off in winter. There are also wide eaves to keep the rain or snow off the outer walls. The roof is made of shingles, which are small overlapping rectangular pieces of wood.

A special kind of frame, rather like a balcony, runs round the front and sides of each house. This frame supports a row

A village church in Slovenia. Note that the roofs are steeply sloped so that the snow can slide off in winter

of horizontal wooden rungs. These rungs are used for drying hay and crops such as maize which have been grown lower down the valley.

The whole of the ground floor of the house is used as a cellar for storing wine, fruit and food. The living quarters are on the first floor. There is a small kitchen with an iron stove, a table

70

and a stool. Next to it is the bedroom. There are three or four bunks in this room and low chests with panels of carved wood in which the clothes are kept. A sheepskin rug covers the floor. The remaining room is a living-room, simply furnished with an oak table, several benches and one or two wicker armchairs. The attic is used as a bedroom for guests.

The Slovene villagers work hard to make a living because crops do not grow well in the stony fields. They also keep dairy cattle, sheep and goats. Some villagers are skilled craftsmen, making furniture and carving souvenirs out of wood for visiting tourists. Others work as wood-cutters, for the valley is rich in valuable softwoods.

Cities and Towns

Many of Yugoslavia's northern towns resemble European ones, especially those of Germany and Austria. Others, in Bosnia and the south, are Turkish or Oriental in appearance. But most Yugoslav towns and cities have a mixture of European and Turkish buildings which is to be found only in the Balkans. The capital of Yugoslavia, Belgrade, is such a city.

Belgrade was founded by Illyrian fishermen, on the banks of the Danube and Sava rivers, long before the Romans came and settled. The Roman engineers built straight roads and paved them with slabs of stone. They built baths and villas. In the fourth century A.D. the Huns occupied the settlement and killed many of its inhabitants, leaving smoke and ruins behind them. But the settlement survived. Then, in the seventh century A.D., the Slavs arrived. They called the settlement Beli Grad, or "the White City", because of its many white houses. With time, the name was changed to Beograd, or Belgrade.

As more and more Slavs came and settled in Belgrade the city spread along the banks of the Danube and Sava. Trade flourished because the city was on important trade routes to the Black Sea and Constantinople. In the thirteenth and fourteenth centuries Belgrade belonged to Hungary.

A few centuries later, in 1521, the Turks besieged and captured Belgrade. They ruled there for nearly 350 years and

Kalemegdan Fortress, with the River Sava in the background

A view of the new part of Belgrade, the capital of Yugoslavia

called the city Darod i Zhihad, or "Home of the Holy Wars".
They built a beautiful mosque with a great dome and slender
towers. They also built a strong fortress called Kalemegdan
from which they guarded the approaches to the city. Today
the Kalemegdan Fortress is a most interesting museum.

But Belgrade is not only a city of historical interest; it is also
the centre of Yugoslavia's administrative and commercial life.
The Yugoslav Head of State has his residence in Belgrade and
the Federal Government have their offices there. The University of Belgrade, which was founded in 1863, is the most
famous in the whole of Yugoslavia.

The city has a population of over 1,200,000, and it continues
to grow. Many of its inhabitants work in the new engineering,

73

chemical and textile factories. Belgrade is an important centre of communications. Railways and roads connect it with all parts of Yugoslavia. Its harbour, on the Danube, has been widened and equipped with modern cranes, warehouses and silos for storing grain.

Many farmers come to Belgrade to sell their produce. The cobbled squares of the city's suburbs are filled with stalls selling an assortment of goods—vegetables, boots, shoes, hand-made toys, pots and pans, skins, belts and saddles.

A street market where vegetables and fruit are sold. The stall-holder is wearing national costume

Housewives can also buy dairy products, poultry and meat from the stalls.

Zagreb, the capital of Croatia, lies on the left bank of the Sava River. It is a well-planned city with straight roads and wide squares suitable for modern traffic. There is a university, in addition to various technical schools and colleges. The centre of the city is attractive with smart shops, hotels and restaurants. It has a population of nearly 763,000.

Zagreb's most famous church is the Catholic Cathedral, which dates back to the thirteenth century. With its twin towers and huge portals it is an imposing building. Inside, there are some beautiful stained-glass windows.

Zagreb is one of the most important industrial and trading centres in Croatia. It has rail and road communications with all parts of Yugoslavia. The legendary Orient Express used to stop at Zagreb on its way to Belgrade and Constantinople. The output from the Zagreb factories is sent by road and railway to the port of Rijeka for export.

Ljubljana, too, is situated near the Sava River. It is the capital of Slovenia and Yugoslavia's third largest city. It dates back to pre-Roman times, and became an important garrison town under the Romans. Today Ljubljana has all the appearance of a modern industrial city. Its mills and factories are supplied with power from hydro-electric stations which have been built to harness the energy from the swift mountain torrents which flow into the Sava. Its population is over 250,000.

The centre of Ljubljana—famous for its dignified university and other historic buildings

Dubrovnik is situated in a beautiful sheltered bay on the central Adriatic coast. The city was founded by Roman and Slav settlers in the seventh century A.D. It became a fortified town in the Middle Ages to protect its citizens from the raids of Saracen and Bulgar pirates, and still has many of its medieval walls. The city was ruled by Venice, the famous Italian City State, for many years before the Hungarians conquered it.

The old city has narrow, flagstoned streets, palaces with ornamental arches, built by Venetian architects, and several fine churches. Dubrovnik's harbour and modern port installations handle ocean-going ships. Many of the inhabitants are employed in the tourist industry and the timber trade, and in the chemical factories. Dubrovnik is the chief port for the export of Dalmatia's farm produce and has a population of about 50,000.

Split lies in a wide bay on the Adriatic coast north of Dubrovnik. The city was founded by the Romans and is famous for the ruins of the beautiful palace built there by the Emperor Diocletian at the end of the third century A.D. Later in its history, Split belonged to Venice.

A view of Dubrovnik. The mediaeval walls, which were built to protect the people from pirates' raids, can be seen clearly in this picture

Today, the city has a population of about 185,000. In summer
its streets are packed with holiday-makers for it is a popular
seaside resort. Split's hotels look out on the blue Adriatic Sea
and the offshore islands. Besides the tourist industry, the city
derives its income from cement factories, paper mills, engineering works and shipyards. There is a busy harbour where
fishing-boats call. The fishermen come to sell their catches in
the central fish market.

Now let's visit Nis, in central Serbia. The town is situated
on a small plain alongside the Morava River in the wide
Morava valley. It is surrounded by gently sloping hills. The

78

countryside around is rich in tobacco plantations and vine-yards.

Nis was once called Nissopolis. The Roman Emperor Constantine was born here in A.D. 273. The Crusaders used the city as a resting-place on their way to the Holy Land. It is thought that Richard Cœur de Lion passed through Nis on his way home from the Crusades.

Today Nis has a population of over 193,000 and is an important railway junction. The town is expanding rapidly and new blocks of flats and factories have been built there recently. One of the largest tobacco factories in Yugoslavia is at Nis. There are also textile mills, chemical factories, cement works and breweries.

Education

All Yugoslav schools are free, and are run by the State. Boys and girls start elementary school when they are eight. They must stay on at school until they are sixteen, and then they may either start work or continue their studies.

Those who wish to continue their studies go to secondary

Yugoslav school children in a remote village

schools or to one of the various types of technical school. One type of secondary school is called the "gymnasium" and entry is selective. This means that boys and girls must pass an entrance examination if they wish to enter the school.

Some pupils leave the gymnasium before reaching the top form and take a special course at a technical school or college which will fit them for a skilled job in industry or commerce.

But pupils completing their course at the gymnasium go on to university. (There are seven universities in Yugoslavia, the most famous being in Belgrade and Zagreb.)

There is no morning assembly in Yugoslav schools and no prayers are said, because all religion and religious instruction is banned. (This is because of the official attitude of the State but many people in Yugoslavia still retain their religious beliefs, particularly in the country areas.) Catholic children may, however, attend special Sunday schools. No religious holidays are observed—children actually go to school on Christmas Day! Instead of Christmas, they celebrate New

These young apprentices are being trained at a centre run by a steel factory in Slovenia. When they have completed the course they will be qualified to take skilled jobs in the steel industry

Year's Day. There are no half-term holidays, but the summer holidays last for over two months.

Pupils in all Yugoslav schools, from the very youngest to those at university, are encouraged to believe in socialism and communism. Every pupil has to learn the history of these movements. And every Yugoslav boy and girl has to belong to the Pioneer Movement (which has been modelled on that of the U.S.S.R.). Pioneers are rather like boy scouts or girl guides. They wear a red scarf and are expected to set a good example, to help their neighbours and to serve their country. Pioneers have their own holiday camps, which they run themselves. At one camp in Belgrade, the children have a miniature railway which links the camp with public transport services. They also produce and print their own magazine.

We have learned that there are three official languages in Yugoslavia. If you went to school in Slovenia your text-books would be written in Slovene in Latin characters, although you would have to learn the Cyrillic alphabet and the Serbo-Croat and Macedonian languages as well. So you would grow up learning three languages and two different alphabets.

Children living in out-of-the-way places, in the mountains and forests of Bosnia or Montenegro, have no schools near their homes. They often have to walk long distances to the nearest village to attend school. In winter, when there is deep snow on the ground, and wolves roam the countryside, the children stay at home. Because of this, they grow up unable to read or write. Fortunately, there are not many children in

82

Pioneers on duty at the holiday camp near Belgrade where the boys and girls run their own railway

this position, and there will be even fewer in the future, for the government is planning to build new schools in these remote areas.

Many schools have television sets and radios, to receive special schools programmes. The programmes are broadcast in the official language of each Republic, for all the Republics have their own radio station and television centre, situated in the capital.

Yugoslav schools close for the summer holidays in about mid-June and do not re-open until September. During their long summer holidays, village children help their parents with haymaking and harvesting. They also look after the sheep and cattle, which are put out into the fields after the wheat has been cut. Some older pupils and students take jobs on farms and are paid like any other worker. Others are lucky enough to find work at the seaside resorts on the Adriatic coast where the tourists from other countries come for their holidays. The students work as waiters, bar stewards or beach attendants, and are paid well.

Sports, Entertainments and Festivals

Yugoslav children play many games. The boys like football, which is played on a hard pitch; and they are keen supporters of their football clubs which have taken part in the European and world championships. Volley-ball and basket-ball are

A game of basket-ball in progress. Although this game was introduced into Yugoslavia quite recently, it has already become popular

played, and school teams compete with one another in the Republic championships. Tennis is a popular game, and is played on hard courts. There are many tennis clubs in the north of the country and on the Adriatic coast, but tennis is never played on grass courts.

The Yugoslavs are extremely keen on athletics. All the larger schools have a sports field where boys and girls practise sprinting, hurdling, the high jump and the long jump, javelin-

A wild boar,
one of the wild
animals the
Yugoslavs like
to hunt

throwing and other athletic sports. Athletes train seriously from an early age, hoping to be selected for the Olympic teams. In 1984 the Winter Olympics were successfully held at Sarajevo, and seen by television viewers all over the world.

Fishing is popular, perhaps because the country has so many mountain streams, lakes and rivers. Groups of boys can sometimes be seen building a dam of twigs and branches across a small river. They leave an opening, and fix a net across it. Then they drive the fish down the river and into the net by beating the water with sticks.

Yugoslavs often go hunting, particularly in the hills and forests of Bosnia and Serbia where foxes, brown bears, deer and wild boar can be found.

From the beginning of December, when the cold and snowy winter sets in, boys and girls can be seen skating on ponds and lakes near their homes. Tennis courts in big cities and resorts are turned into open-air ice-rinks and children learn figure-skating and ice-dancing.

86

The Yugoslavs are an artistic people. They love folk music and dancing. Traditional Yugoslav folk dances are colourful and elaborate. They are based on fairy-tales and have been passed down from generation to generation. The professional dance troupes draw large audiences. The people love to see the dancers stamp and twirl. A favourite dance is the *kola* where the performers link arms or clasp hands, forming a circle round a group of musicians. The best folk dancers have also been trained in ballet. They often give performances abroad and are well paid.

This man is carrying an ancient Slav musical instrument called a gusle

It is usual to have folk dancing and music both at weddings and at the festivals of patron saints. At wedding celebrations, the bridegroom and his bride start the dancing, which is very gay and accompanied by clapping and laughter. The festival of a patron saint is called a *slava*. All the people parade in the streets at these festivals. The men wear white shirts, richly embroidered waistcoats, tight-fitting black trousers and crimson pill-box hats worked with embroidery. The women wear petticoats edged with white lace, brightly-coloured aprons trimmed with gold, blouses of pure silk and bonnets with little silver bells and coloured ribbons.

The most important event in a *slava* is the procession to the church. Carts, drawn by horses or oxen, are decorated with

Skiing is just one of the many ways in which the Yugoslavs take advantage of their cold and snowy winters

Dancing is a favourite entertainment of the Yugoslavs. The crowd watch enthusiastically while this troupe of folk dancers stamp and leap to the rhythm of the drum

flowers, leaves, coloured paper and ribbons. Behind the carts walk the menfolk carrying banners and crosses. The women follow with children holding candles. After church the people feast for hours and dance the traditional dances to the music of fiddles, flutes and accordians.

The Arts

The greatest works of art in Yugoslavia are the beautiful paintings to be found in the churches and monasteries of

Serbia and Macedonia. Many of the paintings are frescoes—that is, they are painted on walls. Although they date from the Middle Ages they are well preserved and still retain their vivid colours. Some illustrate scenes from the Bible and the life of Jesus Christ; others are portraits of saints, kings and princes. Frescoes dating from the eleventh century have been found on the walls of a small monastery two or three miles from the city of Skopje in Macedonia. These frescoes are considered by experts to be the most precious in the whole of Yugoslavia.

Medieval church artists also painted religious pictures on pieces of wood or glass or metal. These pictures are called "icons". Usually they portray the face of Jesus Christ or the faces of saints, or scenes from the Bible. They are hung on the walls of chapels and churches. Orthodox believers pray in front of them. Some icons are believed to work miracles and are worshipped by pilgrims. Nowadays, icons are recognized as works of art, as well as religious objects, and collectors pay high prices for them.

Modern Yugoslav artists make glazed pottery, which they decorate with intricate designs; they are also expert wood-carvers. The women are skilled in delicate embroidery and lace-making; and they weave carpets and rugs as well as embroidering tapestries. At Easter they paint eggs in traditional patterns of flowers or leaves—a custom which goes back many centuries.

Yugoslavia in the Modern World

Marshal Josip Broz Tito ruled Yugoslavia as a Federal Republic from 1945 until his death in May 1980. He held the office of President for life. He was also Commander-in-Chief of the armed forces. Although he was a Communist leader, the system of government he created was different from that of other Communist countries where everything is nationalized or controlled by the State, and no private businesses of any kind are allowed. In Yugoslavia, industry is run partly on Communist lines and partly on capitalist lines. Transport, banking and many industries have been nationalized. But some private businesses are still permitted. People can own workshops and produce goods for profit. Foreign

The seat of the Federal Executive Council of the Yugoslav Government in Belgrade—a new building for a modern nation

firms are able to build factories or hotels in Yugoslavia and make profit on the money they have invested. But if a Yugoslav factory fails to pay its way, the State orders it to be shut down and the workers to be dismissed.

In her foreign policy, also, Yugoslavia pursues an independent course. She co-operates and trades with both Communist and capitalist nations, but she remains neutral. She does not give her support to either side. Like Sweden, India and many African and Asian countries, Yugoslavia belongs to the group of "non-committed" nations.

After the Second World War, Marshal Tito was the chief planner of Yugoslavia's industrial development and foreign policy. All books and newspaper articles which criticized Tito and his party were banned. Even now, only Yugoslavs who support the government are given important jobs in the civil service and in industry. But Yugoslav workers are allowed to travel abroad and many go as migrant workers to West Germany. They then return home in cars laden with refrigerators, washing-machines and other goods.

All this seems strange to us. People who belong to a democratic country, as we do, have the right to criticize their government when they make a mistake. They enjoy hearing or watching politicians from different parties argue on radio or television about the best way to solve social and national problems. They do not like to belong to a political party merely in order to secure a good job, as the Yugoslavs have to do.

92

New schools are being built in all parts of the country to educate children such as these for their important role as Yugoslavia's future citizens

And yet, today, the Yugoslav nation is shaping itself into a modern industrial society. The people are working hard to develop their heavy industries, their electricity, oil and gas resources, their transport and farming. The industrial progress made by Yugoslavia since the end of the Second World War has been so great that her people now enjoy the highest standard of living of any country in the Balkans.

93

Index

95